The Gardener's Tale

Contents

The Gardener's Tale

Brandon Robshaw
and
Rochelle Scholar

Published in association with
The Basic Skills Agency

Acknowledgements
Illustrations: Juan Hayward.
Cover: Juan Hayward.

Orders: please contact Bookpoint Ltd, 39 Milton Park, Abingdon, Oxon OX14
4TD. Telephone: (44) 01235 400414, Fax: (44) 01235 400454. Lines are open
from 9.00–6.00, Monday to Saturday, with a 24 hour message answering service.
Email address: orders@bookpoint.co.uk

British Library Cataloguing in Publication Data
A catalogue record for this title is available from The British Library

ISBN 0 340 72098 0

First published 1998
Impression number   10 9 8 7 6 5 4 3 2
Year   2003 2002 2001 2000 1999

Typeset by Fakenham Photosetting Ltd, Fakenham, Norfolk.
Printed in Great Britain for Hodder & Stoughton Educational, a division of
Hodder Headline Plc, 338 Euston Road, London NW1 3BH by Athenaeum Press
Ltd, Gateshead, Tyne & Wear.

1

Jim and Sue

Jim Brown was a big, fat bloke
who liked a good laugh.
He liked going ten-pin bowling
with his mates, telling jokes
and having a few beers.

He always seemed to be happy.
But Jim was not happy.
Not all the time anyway.

He was often unhappy,
because he was in love.
He was in love with a woman
who did not love him.

Her name was Sue – Sue Fox.
He saw her a lot because she lived
in the same road as him.
She shopped in the same shops.
So Jim saw a lot of her.
They always stopped
for a chat when they met.
She was always friendly.
She seemed to like him.
But Jim knew she didn't love him.

Maybe not everyone would call her beautiful.
But to Jim, she was so beautiful
it gave him a pain.
He wanted to fall on the ground
when he saw her.
But he just grinned and said 'hello'.

He told his mates about her one night,
down at the bowling alley.
Of course,
he made a bit of a joke out of it.
That was Jim all over –
making a joke out of everything.

'I'm so crazy about her I'm wasting away!',
he said. 'I'm losing weight. Soon I'll be
as thin as a rake.'

His friends looked at his big fat belly
and laughed.
'Why don't you ask her out?' asked Dave.
'No, I couldn't,' said Jim.
'Why not?' asked Dave.
'Because she might say "no",' Jim replied.
'But isn't it worth a try?' Dave asked.

Jim shook his head.
He changed the subject.

'If I get a strike with this ball,
will you get me a coke?'
'You won't get a strike,' said Dave.
'Oh, won't I?' said Jim. 'Watch.'

He bowled the ball at the skittles.
It hit them on one side
and five fell over.

'Five,' said Dave, 'that's only half a strike!'
'Buy me half a coke then!' said Jim.

His friends laughed.
But Jim started to play better.
He won every game he played,
and went home in a good mood.

He started to change his mind.
Maybe it was a good idea to ask Sue out.
Maybe she would say 'yes'.

He decided – next time he saw Sue,
he would ask her out.

2

The Gardener's Work

Jim worked in the local park
as a gardener.
He thought about Sue
at work all the next day.
He thought about her
as he pulled up the weeds.
He thought about her as he
dug the flower beds.
He thought about her
as he watered the cricket pitch.

He thought about her smile.
He thought about her laugh.
He thought about her long brown hair.
In the end, he just stopped working.
He just wanted to think about Sue.
He leaned on his spade
and smoked a cigarette.

It was a sunny day and Jim felt happy.
His head was full of thoughts of Sue.
He would ask her out, and she would say 'yes'.
He would be the happiest man alive.

'Brown!' said a loud, angry voice.
'What do you think you're doing?'

It was the voice of
the Parks Inspector, Mr Gitting.
He was a short, thin man with
a black cap and a black moustache.
None of the gardeners liked him much.
He was always shouting at them.
Always trying to catch them out.

'What are you doing?' said Mr Gitting again.

'I was having a rest,' said Jim.

'It's not your break!' shouted Mr Gitting,
'You shouldn't be resting.'

'I was having a fag break,' said Jim.

'Well, you're not allowed fag breaks,'
shouted Mr Gitting. 'Put it out now!'

'Sorry,' said Jim.

'You will be sorry if
I catch you slacking again,' said Mr Gitting.

Jim picked up his spade.
He got back to work,
and Mr Gitting walked away.

A bit later, Jim looked up to see
if Mr Gitting was still around.
He wasn't, but Jim saw someone else.

It was a woman. She was walking
across the park towards Jim.
Jim's heart started to beat faster.
The woman was Sue Fox.

3

In the Park

'Hello Jim,' said Sue. 'Nice day.'
'Hello Sue,' said Jim. 'Yes it is a nice day.'

He grinned at her.
'Where are you going?' he asked.
'I've got a new job in a supermarket,'
said Sue, 'I start today.'
'That's good,' said Jim, 'Good luck with it.'
'Thanks,' said Sue.

Jim couldn't think of anything else to say.
'Goodbye then,' said Sue.
She started to walk away.

'Wait!' said Jim.
'What is it?' Sue asked.
'There is something I want to tell you,'
said Jim.
'What is it?' asked Sue.

'Well . . .' said Jim.
His heart was beating fast.
His mouth felt dry.
'There were these two cows in a field.
And one cow said to the other:
"Aren't you afraid of this Mad Cow Disease?"
And the other cow said:
"It doesn't worry me – I'm a tractor!" '

Sue laughed. 'Good joke,' she said.
'I will tell it to the girls at work.
Well, I must go now. Goodbye.'
'Goodbye,' said Jim.

He watched her walk away across the park.
He felt very angry with himself.
Why hadn't he asked her out?
Why had he told her that stupid joke instead?

He stood there sadly, thinking about
the chance he had missed.

'Brown!' said a loud angry voice.
It was Mr Gitting again.
'You're slacking!'

'Sorry Mr Gitting,' said Jim.
'If I catch you slacking one more time,
you will get the sack,' said Mr Gitting.

Jim sighed and got back to work.
He was not having a good day.

4

At the Bowling Alley

That night, Jim went to the bowling alley.

His mate Dave was there.

They had a few games together.

Jim started telling jokes.

'This horse goes into the pub,' he said,
'It asks for a beer. The barman says,
"Certainly, sir. But why the long face?" '

'Ha, ha,' said Dave. 'That's not bad.
But Jim, you've got a bit of
a long face yourself. What's the matter?'

'I saw Sue Fox today,' said Jim.
'What happened?' asked Dave.

'I wanted to ask her out,' said Jim,
'But it didn't go right.'

'What did you say to her?' asked Dave.
'I told her a joke,' Jim replied.
'Oh no,' said Dave, 'that was stupid.'

'All right,' said Jim, 'I know it was stupid.
But I couldn't help it.
I lost my nerve.'
He took out a cigarette.
'Have you got a light?'

'Here,' said Dave, 'Listen, I've got a plan.'
'You've got a plan?' asked Jim.
'Yes,' said Dave, 'I'm a man with a plan.'

'Well what is it then?' asked Jim.
'Have a few drinks before
you speak to her again,' said Dave.
'Then you'll feel relaxed.
It will be easy to ask her out.'

'You mean I should get drunk?' asked Jim.
'Well, just a bit merry –
it will make you relaxed.'
'All right,' said Jim, 'I'll try it.
It might work.'

'Now is your chance,' said Dave,
'Don't look now, but she's just walked in.'

5

Disaster Strikes

Jim started to turn around.
Dave gave him a kick.
'Don't look now,' he said, 'Play it cool.
Go to the bar and buy a drink.'
'All right,' said Jim, 'I'll have a coke.'
He was so nervous he felt sick.

'Don't be stupid,' said Dave. 'That won't
make you drunk. I will get you a beer.
That will do the trick.'

Jim drank the beer. And another.

And then another.

He started to feel very relaxed.

It was half past ten.

He looked round and saw Sue.

She was in the next lane.

She was playing against a young man

Jim had never seen before.

Jim drank his last pint very quickly.
Then he got up
and walked over to Sue's lane.
She was sitting at a table,
talking to the young man.

'Hello, Jim,' said Sue. 'This is Nick.'

'Hello, Nick,' said Jim.
'Sue, I want to tell you a joke.
There was this bloke, and one day,
he woke up with an elephant.
Or was it a camel? No, that's not right.
He woke up in bed with a giraffe,
and the giraffe said . . . No, wait a minute,
it was a hippo. No, that's not right . . .'

Jim couldn't remember the joke.
His voice sounded thick and far away.
He was swaying from side to side.
He was drunk.

'I love you Sue,' he said.
'I love you, but I feel sick.'
He ran into the toilet.
When he came out, he looked around for Sue.
But she was gone.

'Where is she?' he asked Dave.
'She left,' said Dave.
'She left with Nick.'

6

The Morning
After

The next day, Jim woke up in bed
with a sore head.
His mouth was dry. He didn't feel too good.
Something was worrying him.
At first, he couldn't think what it was,
but then it all came back to him.
The bowling alley. Drinking too much.
Sue sitting there with her friend Nick.
Telling Sue he loved her.
Running to the toilet to be sick.

'Oh no!' Jim groaned to himself.
'I've made a right fool of myself.'

What would Sue think of him now?
He didn't want to see her.
He felt too ashamed.

He got up and got ready for work.
He did everything very slowly,
because his head was hurting.
But the pain in his head was nothing.
It was the pain in his heart
that really hurt.

When he got to work, Mr Gitting
was waiting for him.
'You're late, Brown,' he said.
'I've got my eye on you. I'm watching you.
I want you to edge the grass today.
And if you slack, you get the sack.'

Jim picked up his tools and got to work,
edging the grass.

As he worked, he thought about Sue.
What would he say if he saw her?

And then he did see her.
She was walking across the park with Nick.
They were chatting together.
Nick put his arm around Sue.
A cold feeling ran through Jim's guts.
Was Nick Sue's new boyfriend?
He couldn't stand it. It was too much.

Jim threw down his spade
and went over to them.

'Look,' he said. 'I'm sorry about last night.
I had a bit too much to drink.'
'That's all right,' said Sue.
'But,' said Jim, 'who is
this bloke you're with?'

'I'm Nick,' said Nick.
'I'm not talking to you,' said Jim,
'I'm talking to Sue, all right?
Sue, why are you going around
with this Nick?
He is not the right one for you.'

'Jim, don't be silly,' said Sue.
'I'm not being silly,' said Jim.
'Don't call me silly. You're the silly one,
if you go around with this Nick bloke.'

'Come on,' said Sue to Nick, 'Let's go.'
They started walking away.

'Sue!' shouted Jim. 'Don't walk away!
Don't go off with that stupid Nick!
He's a waste of space!'

But Sue and Nick
just carried on walking away.

'Brown!' said a voice.

It was the voice of Mr Gitting.

'What are you doing?

I find you shouting at people
instead of working.

You have thrown down your tools.

You are not edging the grass,
you are shouting at people instead!

We don't pay you to shout at people.

Well, this time you have gone too far.

You are sacked!'

7

What Now?

So now Jim had lost everything.
He had lost his job.
He had lost his last chance
of going out with Sue.
Everything had gone wrong.
And the trouble was,
there was no-one to blame but himself.

He went to see his mate Dave that evening.
Perhaps Dave would cheer him up.

Jim always tried to be cheerful,
even when everything had gone wrong.

'Here's a joke,' he said to Dave.
'A man walked into a bar.
He woke up two days later
with a lump on his head.
It was a metal bar.'

'That's an old joke,' said Dave,
'I've heard it before, about 20 times.'

'Oh well,' said Jim.
He couldn't think of any more jokes.
Suddenly, he felt very, very sad.

'I lost my job today,' he told Dave.
'That's bad,' said Dave.
'I know,' said Jim. 'And I made a fool of
myself with Sue in the park.
I shouted at her new boyfriend, Nick.'

'That's bad, too.'
'I know it's bad,' said Jim.
'It's so bad it's driving me mad.'

'What are you going to do?' asked Dave.
'I don't know,' said Jim.
'I can't do anything about Sue. After today,
she will never speak to me again.
But I must find another job.'
'What job will you do?' asked Dave.

Jim thought about it.
What job could he do?
He had never passed any exams.
He couldn't be a doctor or a teacher
or a lawyer. He couldn't be a dentist
or a chemist or a journalist.
The only thing he had experience of
was gardening.
And now he couldn't even do that.

'I don't know,' he said.

'I just don't know.'

'Go down to the Job Centre,' said Dave.

'Maybe you'll find something there.'

'Maybe I will,' said Jim.

'I hope so,' said Dave.

'So do I,' said Jim, 'So do I.'

8

Experience
Required

The Job Centre had lots of cards
in the window.
It looked to Jim as if there were
a lot of job vacancies.
Inside there were even more.

But there was just one problem.
When you looked closely at the cards,
they all said the same thing:
Experience required.

Over and over again, those same two words –
Experience required. Experience required.
Experience required.

Van driver wanted, experience required.
Secretary wanted, experience required.
Builder's mate wanted, experience required.
Plumber's mate wanted, experience required.
Computer programmer wanted,
experience required.

Jim went to talk to the woman at the desk.
'How do you get experience?' he asked her.
'You have to get a job,' she replied.
'And how do you get a job?' Jim asked.
'You need experience,' said the woman.

It was like a joke.
The problem was, it wasn't a joke.
It was true.

Jim couldn't stand it any more.
He walked out of the Job Centre.

It was lunch time and he was getting hungry.
He made up his mind to go to the supermarket
in the High Street and buy some sausages.
Then he would go home and cook them.
Some nice sausages would cheer him up.

He got a packet of sausages
and put it in his basket.
He also got some potatoes and onions.
He filled up his basket with
a loaf of bread, a pint of milk
and a packet of tea.
Now he could have a nice lunch.

He joined the queue for the check-out.
It was not until he got to the front
of the queue that he saw who was on the till.

It was Sue Fox.

9

Friends Again

Jim didn't know what to say.
He just stood there grinning like a fool.
Sue looked at him.
Then she said, 'Hello, Jim.'
Jim was thankful that she was still
speaking to him.
She sounded quite friendly.

'Hello, Sue,' said Jim.
'Nice day for the race.'
'Race? What race?'
'The human race!' said Jim.

Sue smiled at this joke.
Jim was glad to see her smile.
She had a wonderful smile.
At least they could still be friends.
That was something.

'I'm very sorry for shouting at you
in the park,' he said. 'And for shouting
at Nick. Say sorry to him for me, will you?'
'All right,' said Sue.
'And now let's forget about it.'
'OK,' said Jim. He felt much better
now he had said sorry.

'Did you get in trouble with your boss?'
asked Sue. 'I saw him having a go at you.'
'Yes,' said Jim. 'I got the sack.'
'You got the sack?' said Sue. 'That's awful.'

'I know,' said Jim.

'And now I need another job.'

'There's a vacancy here,' said Sue.

'A vacancy?' said Jim.

'Yes,' said Sue, 'A vacancy

for a check-out person.'

'I've got no experience,' said Jim.

'That doesn't matter,' said Sue.

'You can learn on the job.

Look, there's the manager over there.

Why don't you go and see her about it?'

'Right,' said Jim, 'I will.'

10

The Happiest
Man Alive

'Excuse me,' said Jim.
'Yes?' said the manager.
She was a middle-aged woman
with curly blonde hair.
She wore a name badge that said
'Mrs Johnson.'

'It's about the job vacancy, Mrs Johnson,'
said Jim. 'For the check-out person.'

Mrs Johnson looked surprised.
'But you're a man!' she said.
'Yes,' said Jim, 'At least I was
the last time I looked.'

Mrs Johnson looked at him.
Then she laughed. 'All right,' she said.
'I'll give you a try.
Have you worked on a till before?'
'No,' said Jim. 'But I want to learn.'

'You can start tomorrow,' said Mrs Johnson.
'We open at nine o'clock.
Come in at eight for training.'

Jim did not find the training too hard.
At nine o'clock, he was on the till,
serving his first customer.
The work was very tiring,
but the morning went quickly.

Jim was glad when it was eleven o'clock.
Eleven o'clock was the time for his break.
He left his till and went to the tea room.

He was glad to see that Sue was there.
She was having her break too.
He went and sat with her.
She smiled at him.

'I'm glad you got the job,' she said.
'So am I!' said Jim.

How nice she was, he thought.
He wanted to say something to show
that there were no hard feelings about Nick.
That he was still Sue's friend.

'How is Nick?' he said.
'He had a good time,' said Sue.
'He's gone back to New Zealand now.'
'What?' said Jim.
He could not believe his ears.

'He's gone back to New Zealand,' Sue said.
'He is my brother. He lives in New Zealand.
He was here on a visit.'
'Your brother?' said Jim. 'But why
didn't you tell me he was your brother?'

Sue smiled. 'You were a bit rude to me
in the park. I thought I would teach you
a lesson.'

'So – you haven't got anyone?' said Jim.
'A partner, I mean. You're on your own,
like me.'
'I might be,' said Sue.
'Might be?' asked Jim.

'I might be on my own,' said Sue.
'It depends if you say "yes"
when I ask you out.'
'What?'
'I'm asking you out,' said Sue.

'What is it – yes or no?'
'It's yes, of course!' said Jim.
'Yes! Yes! Yes!'

'Where shall we go?'
'Don't know,' said Jim.
'I know,' said Sue, 'We'll buy some food
from the supermarket. Then when it closes,
we'll go for a picnic in the park
where you used to work.'

It was a wonderful idea.
It would make Mr Gitting very angry,
to see the two of them sitting in his park,
eating food and drinking wine.

Jim went back to his till
with a big smile on his face.
Sue, the woman he loved,
had asked him out.
She had asked him out, and he had said 'yes'.

He was the happiest man alive.